Berlin

AKNOWLEDGEMENTS

I would like to thank the many German and foreign architects working in Berlin, whom I interviewed or whose buildings I reviewed over the last twelve years, and Christoph Krämer and Herman L. Gremliza, chief editor of *Konkret*, for their thought-provoking discussions.

This edition published by Carlton Publishing Group 2002
20 Mortimer Street
London
W1T 3JW

A CIP catalogue for this book is available from the British Library.

ISBN 1 84222 637 1

Commissioning Editor: Claire Richardson
Design: Adam Wright/Simon Mercer
Picture research: Claire Gouldstone
Production: Janette Burgin

Printed in Dubai

Berlin

LAYLA DAWSON

Berlin

is Bertolt Brecht, Marlene Dietrich, Christopher Isherwood and John Le Carré. It is political theatre, soldiers and spies, a city that has only recently come in from the cold. Germany arrived late on the world stage of nations and Berlin has only been its national capital since 1871. It is as divided in its position astride two rivers, the Spree and Havel, as it is between its authoritarian and subversive tendencies. As intellectual meeting point between Moscow and Paris it has been sensitive to every ideology, the staging point for two world wars, a forty-five year political ice age that teetered on the edge of nuclear war, a sudden turn of events which left politicians fumbling for their scripts and European reunification. Following every explosion Berlin has reinvented itself in new architecture. Kaisers, a fascist dictator, two opposing regimes, and a born-again democracy have tried to hide their inferiority complexes under bombastic architectural manners. The result has been a metropolitan game of musical chairs in which buildings have housed diametrically opposed political masters in quick succession.

Between 1945 and 1990 East Berlin was the capital of the socialist German Democratic Republic (GDR), and West Berlin an outpost colony of booming capitalist Federal Republic of Germany (FRG). In the power vacuum between November 1989 and 1990 the metropole achieved fame as the capital of Techno music. Young music entrepreneurs took over a bank vault, abandoned in no-mans land since 1945, that could only be reached through a street manhole. Artists occupied Tacheles, the ruined remains of Alfred Messel's 1904 Wertheim department store in Oranienburger Strasse, turning it into an alternative culture venue. All too quickly however, after official reunification in 1990, high finance and developers moved into the wastelands on both sides of the demilitarised zone, turning them into dust bowls of building activity. Streets were renamed in keeping with the new world order and whole new districts were created. Berliners were unable to recognise their own city. The *Falk Berlin by Car* city map was being revised every ten to eighteen months and taxi drivers were loathe to cross into unknown territory. Even now the city remains deeply divided, although the wall has vanished. Berlin's schizophrenia is both magnetic and depressive. If stones could speak the cacophony would be deafening.

The most positive aspects of Berlin's architecture are represented by two buildings; Karl Friedrich Schinkel's 1828 Altes Museum and Mies van der Rohe's 1968 Neue Nationalgalerie. These two bridge the historical abyss between Berlin's "age of enlightenment" and its post-fascist return to civilisation. Both architects employed the rules of classical Greek proportions, each in the spirit of their age. Schinkel, the greatest German architect of the nineteenth century, was a Prussian influenced by Italy and France and interested in England's industrial developments. Mies was to transpose Schinkel's Grecian discipline into twentieth century steel and glass and export it to America and the rest of the world. Their aim was not to overawe but to create humane cityscapes that would stimulate and set minds free. In the time between these two constructions however Berlin's architecture was to come under the influence of strong, politically motivated, aesthetic ideologies.

Berlin's historical centre was shaped by Karl Friedrich Schinkel, Carl Gotthard Langhans, Friedrich August Stüler, Georg Wenzeslaus von Knobelsdorff and Johann Boumann from the end of the seventeenth century on into the nineteenth century. This European movement saw rationality as the bedrock of man's relationship with the world and, by means of patronage and competitions, public architecture flourished.

PRE-1939 BERLIN STILL HAD AN homogeneous CITYSCAPE OF **STONE FACADES** AND WIDE STRAIGHT STREETS, COBBLED OR LINED WITH TREES, CULMINATING IN *PLÄTZE*, ROUND, SQUARE OR shapeless TRAFFIC JUNCTIONS OR ORNAMENTAL PARKS.

City blocks of uniform height had vehicle entrances into inner courtyards of lower class flats, private gardens or craftsmens' workshops. High points on the skyline of this densely packed architecture were spires and domes.

At the beginning of the twentieth century architects became professionals and technocrats in a machine age. Clean lines and functionality became paramount in the service of industrialisation. Peter Behrens's 1910 AEG Turbine Factory, as an example of architecture as corporate identity, is a milestone. The future masters of Modernism; Walter Gropius, Mies van der Rohe and Le Corbusier, were all apprentices in Behrens's Berlin studio. Two movements, Expressionism and Modernism, existed side by side. The fluid curves of Erich Mendelsohn's 1924 Einsteinturm developed into his more functional 1930 headquarters for the German metalworkers. Emil Fahrenkamp's 1931 Shellhaus in which functional offices are stepped in waves alongside the Reichpietschufer canal bank is a universally quoted expressionist facade. The 1930s saw the brothers Max and Bruno Taut, Hans Scharoun and Mendelsohn become architects of the boom in industrial headquarters and large scale Berlin workers suburbs, called *Siedlungen*, in Britz, Onkel Toms Hütte and Siemensstadt. The Bauhaus, the world's most influential school of art, design and architecture had been founded in Weimar, and thrived in Dessau from 1926–1933. It found its final refuge in Seglitz, Berlin, in 1933 for only a couple of months before Mies van der Rohe, its last director, and many staff and students, had to flee the fascist regime. It was to be many decades before Scharoun, Gropius, Le Corbusier, Max Taut and Mies would return to Berlin. Some of them would reappear only posthumously, represented by buildings constructed after their death.

The Nazis' era WAS **NOTHING LESS** THAN **A BREAK IN CIVILISATION**.

Many modernist architects and artists were labelled "degenerate" by the National Socialist German Workers Party which ruled from Berlin and had conquered most of Europe between 1933 and 1945. Within the first year all other political parties were dissolved, opponents were imprisoned and workers unions outlawed. The Gestapo was founded and there was a great book burning on Unter den Linden, near the Humboldt University. The last national election took place in 1933 and Adolf Hitler thereafter ruled by decree. Paul Wallot's 1894 Reichstag building, as a parliament, became superfluous and was the victim of arson in 1933. Which political faction was to blame is still debated.

Albert Speer was Hitler's second chief architect after Paul Ludwig Troost died in 1934. Speer was responsible for Berlin planning as general building inspector for the capital between 1937–45. His gargantuan scale re-planning of the capital with neo-classical projects joined up by a grid of streets for marching armies, like the east-west Strasse des 17 Juni as it is now called, was fortunately not completed. Or, like his Chancellery for Hitler on Voss Strasse, was destroyed by bombs. However, the house he designed in 1936 for his close friend, film-maker Leni Riefenstahl, was still mentioned in a footnote to a 1990 Berlin guide book. Military and transport constructions had priority in preparation for war so Tempelhof Airport was enlarged 1936–41 by the air ministry architect Ernst Sagebiel. The most important ensemble built at this time, and still in use, is the 1936 Olympics complex. Werner March designed the thirteen halls, bell tower, great stadium and open-air theatre, with sculptures by Arno Breker. Hitler used this international spectacle and theatrical setting to impress the world, and also lull it into a false sense of security as regards his planned aggressive intentions. Compare March's overwhelming Olympic concept with Langhof Hänni Meerstein's 1987 Spreewald Platz swimming pool and 1990 Horst Korber Sportzentrum, or Dominique Perrault's Prenzlauer Berg velodrome and swim stadium completed after reunification in anticipation of Berlin hosting the 2000 Olympics.

Hitler's allies, the Axis Powers of Italy and Japan, built their embassies respectively in 1939 and 1942 in the leafy Tiergarten diplomatic quarter. Designed by Friedrich Hetzelt and Ludwig Moshammer they are both examples of the lifeless neo-classical style in which Speer hoped to remodel the entire city after Hitler had completed his world domination programme. Both embassies were restored and extended in 2000 for Italy and Japan's present diplomatic delegations to the Berlin Republic.

Although Hitler's seat of government was destroyed during the Battle for Berlin in the last weeks of the war, much early twentieth century modern architecture remained intact in both east and west. However, Berlin's historical centre found itself almost entirely in the Soviet sector. Although US President Kennedy stood on the west side of the Brandenburger Tor to declare "I am a Berliner" (much to the Germans' amusement as this is the name for a jam-filled doughnut), the heart of the city – the Gate leading into Pariser Platz and Unter den Linden, the Platz der Akademie (renamed Gendarmenmarkt in 1990), Friedrichstadt and the island of museums – in the east, was behind the pre-cast concrete wall erected by the GDR in 1961.

Post-war Berlin was cut like a cake, administered by the Soviets in the east and in the west by the Americans, British and French. Wishing to leave their mark on the city that had caused them so much suffering, the Soviets had sculptor J B Belopolski design the rough hewn 1949 Treptow Park memorial for their war dead and in 1953 built an imposing embassy (now the Russian embassy) on Unter den Linden, in official Moscow neo-classical style. With German leaders drawn from returned exiles and concentration camp survivors the Soviets set about creating an alternative Germany, in their own image.

The GDR, as an autonomous East German state with East Berlin as its capital, was founded in 1949. Its first priority was housing. Factory mass production of pre-cast elements cut costs and construction time but left little freedom for design diversity. Not only in dormitory suburbs like Marzhan but also in the inner city high rise slab blocks were hastily built. As finance ran out, the size of the units and amenities, like lifts, were pared down. GDR architecture reflected the state of the nation. Architects had to create more from less and functionality took precedence over aesthetics. The new state, under siege and officially unrecognised by West Germany, felt it had to prove itself. Hermann Henselmann, Berlin's chief architect during most of the GDR's existence, was responsible for three landmarks: the 1950 pastiche classical Palaces for the People apartment blocks along Karl Marx Allee (previously Stalin Allee), which after post reunification renovation are much in demand; the 1969 GDR television tower in Alexander Platz with its revolving steel globe restaurant and his 1964 Haus des Lehrers (Teachers' Building) with Kongresshalle.

Alexander Platz, in contrast to Potsdamer Platz in the west which had been abandoned as a site not worth developing, was remodelled as a public recreation area with entertainment venues and restaurants. This was to be the seed of its downfall on 4 November 1989, because it provided the perfect stage for a final mass demonstration culminating in the GDR's disintegration.

For state ceremonies the GDR had Marx Engels Platz (renamed Platz der Republik in 1990) which was laid out on the site of the 1713 Stadt Schloss. This undistinguished neo-baroque palace had been heavily bombed and was finally demolished in 1950. A modern bronzed glass and concrete Palast der Republik was erected in 1976 on one side of the Platz.

Containing the Volkskammer parliament and public restaurants, it was designed by Heinz Graffunder and Karl-Ernst Swora. However, one portal of the demolished Stadt Schloss – including the balcony from which Karl Liebknecht had proclaimed a short-lived socialist Republic in 1918 – was salvaged to be incorporated into a neighbouring GDR ministry building, now one of the new Berlin Republic's buildings.

Whether the former GDR's Palast der Republik should be allowed to remain, now that its asbestos interiors have been removed, or whether the Stadt Schloss should be resurrected in Disney-style, is part of a wider Berlin debate which has raged since reunification.

THE reconstructionists' nostalgia FOR A PRUSSIAN STONE GRANDEUR IS SEEN BY CRITICS AS A WISH TO REWRITE history.

In 1994 Daniel Libeskind, the American architect who has made Berlin his base since building the Jewish Museum, called the reconstructionists' regressive architectural movement "a call to order in the guise of historical continuity".

In 2000 a government commission was set up to advise on whether a Stadt Schloss facsimile should be built and, if so, for what use. Simultaneously an ideas competition was held for the site. Hamburg architects von Gerkan, Marg and Partner suggested a modern glazed building on which the Stadt Schloss facade would be etched in computer pixels. Sauerbruch Hutton, a Berlin and London practice, designed a cluster of event venues to be related to the existing museum island. Ingenhoven Overdiek and Partner, from Düsseldorf, rejected any architecture and suggested an inner city park. Since then the government commission has tentatively recommended a reconstruction of the palace facade, but applied to the exterior of a modern building. Finance and function need to be decided. One of the arguments for the reconstruction of the Stadt Schloss is that it is the central missing piece in an historical jigsaw, without which the cultural kernel of the city has no focal point. Despite the high quality of contemporary architecture there are obviously some who would prefer a piece of cardboard retro-architecture.

Present-day Berlin benefits from the fact that most of its historic landmarks were on the east side of the Wall. In the communist planned economy there was no pressure to demolish old buildings to make way for profitable commercial premises. Until reunification many stone facades still bore the scars of bullets and shrapnel. The Wall could be said to have preserved some of the city's most valuable architectural treasures.

BUILT BY THE GDR IN THE SUMMER OF **1961**, TO HALT **emigration** TO THE WEST AND CONTROL BLACK MARKETING BETWEEN TWO CURRENCIES, **THE WALL** WAS BERLIN'S MOST **famous** AND **HATED** LANDMARK FOR TWENTY-EIGHT YEARS.

Nothing remains of its 66 miles of concrete, 35 miles of barbed wire and 260 watchtowers encircling West Berlin. Shortly after its fall it was bought up by international dealers, hacked into chunks, and sold as souvenirs. A few panels were still standing beside the Martin Gropius exhibition building in 2001 but those sections with the best graffiti have long gone.

The end of the Second World War did not mean a resumption of normal architectural relations. The sudden construction of the Wall frightened many West Berliners into moving back into what they perceived as the comparative safety of West Germany. From 1939 Berlin was regarded as an increasingly dangerous place to live and the population steadily fell, from four and a half million to three million in 1985. Many businesses left but as a capitalist showcase West Berlin's economy was propped up by subsidies and, as a bonus, West Berlin young men were exempt from military service.

During this Cold War period architecture became just another weapon in a high noon stand-off. Western shop front architecture, constructed as close to the ideological border as possible in order to instil jealousy in the enemy, produced some crass commercial projects. The Springer Publishing House, the object of West Berlin demonstrations against its right-wing editorial stance in the sixties and seventies, made a political decision to build its headquarters in the economically blighted desert next to the Wall in 1966. An unfortunate symbol of West German–American friendship, the 1957 Kongresshalle on John Foster Dulles Allee, was built with a state of the art suspended concrete shell roof which partially collapsed in 1980 and took seven years to restore.

In a higher architectural category, Hans Scharoun designed three pivotal Berlin icons very near the Wall. The Philharmonic Hall (1963), the Kammermusiksaal (1978) and Staatsbibliothek (1987) are free flowing shapes clad in gold anodised, perforated metal plates, which peak across the skyline like expressionist tents (the latter two were completed after his death by pupil Edgar Wisniewski). Designed from the inside outwards, to achieve optimal acoustics, the Philharmonie and Kammermusiksaal are architecture as frozen music. The Staatsbibliothek, with its matching concept of continuous internal space flowing between changing levels, closes the eastern boundary of the Kulturforum, a windswept square which has never lived up to its promise of a vibrant meeting point. The attraction of Hilmer & Sattler's Gemälde Galerie (1998) has not significantly improved its popularity.

Directly opposite Zoo railway station, the arrival point for many tourists, the ruined spire of the bombed 1895 Kaiser Wilhelm Memorial Church was left standing and in 1963 Egon Eiermann added two honeycombed structures with brilliant stained glass as a permanent war memorial. A place of peace and reflection in West Berlin's tumult of chain store consumerism along the Kurfurstendamm it soon became an international back-packers meeting point and was nicknamed the "lipstick".

It was essential during this period that West Berlin should be internationally recognised in order not to be forgotten. The West's answer to Henselmann's Stalin Allee Palaces for the People was the 1957 Interbau IBA, International Building Exhibition. West Berlin must be seen to outdo East Berlin as regards care for its people. Le Corbusier constructed a less successful but virtual copy of his Marseilles Unite d'Habitation in the Westend. While in the Hansaviertel a parkland suburb for 5,000, based on Dutch housing studies by van den Broek and Bakema, was completed by Walter Gropius, Alvar Aalto, Arne Jacobsen, Oscar Niemeyer, Egon Eiermann, and Max Taut, just some of the fifty three architects from thirteen countries taking part.

West Berlin's unique isolation during the Cold War also attracted academic and political tourism. In Brutalist-style concrete Ralf Schüler and Ursulina Schüler-Witte erected their 1979 International Congress Centrum, a colossal machine of a building. Like a serviced satellite town it links up with the existing trade fair grounds and has its own autobahn and rail connections to the west and Tegel (West Berlin airport), so that conference visitors can pop in and out without once having to experience Berlin reality.

National and international institutions were also encouraged to make West Berlin their headquarters, sometimes at considerable cost. The Bauhaus Archives building – an administrator for the licensing of Bauhaus designs, library and exhibition centre – had originally been designed by Walter Gropius, the first Bauhaus School director, for a Darmstadt site in 1964. After his death in 1969 the Archives were persuaded to move to West Berlin and Alexander Cvijanovic had to adapt a building designed for a flat, south-facing aspect in an idyllic landscape, to one for a sloping, urban, north-facing site on Klingelhöferstrasse. It is something to be said for the strength of Gropius' concept and Cvijanovic's sensitivity that the design survived transplantation.

WEST BERLIN'S STATE OF political limbo MADE IT AN undisturbed CORNER FOR EXPERIMENTAL ARCHITECTURE, radical YOUTH AND ALTERNATIVE LIFESTYLES.

In the 1970s Ludwig Leo – described decades later by architect Christoph Langhof as "Berlin student architects' secret hero" – completed two innovative structures: the 1972 DLRG lifesaving association's tower on the Havel, which is shaped by its small site and storage requirements for thirty life boats, and the 1976 Marine and Shipbuilding Institute research plant. In striking pink, blue and green this was early high-tech architecture.

With the 1980s a new era of Post-Modernism, executed by a post-war generation, began to appear in Berlin. This appliqué architecture juggled with a historical mish-mash of materials, columns, colour and symbolism, in an attempt to blur the seams between old and new. Piecemeal infill was favoured over large-scale new estates, in an attempt to win back residential space in the core of the city and repair the traditional Berlin block structure. This culminated in a second major West Berlin International Building Exhibition, the 1987 IBA, in which Rob Krier planned a mixed commercial and residential project in Kreuzberg for young low-income families. His first inner city repair scheme had been completed in Ritterstrasse in

1981. In a similar style Hans Hollein, Giorgio Grassi and Aldo Rossi built apartments, disguised as "city villas", in Rauchstrasse in 1984. Architects were experimenting with more sensual, individualistic forms. Inken and Hinrich Baller developed a filigree architecture in their 1988 Charlottenburg Sporthalle and 1983 Dahlem Philosophisches Institut. James Stirling, the English post modernist, built his first German project, the Wissenschaftszentrum on Reichpietschufer. After Stirling's early death his partner Michael Wilford designed and built Berlin's British Embassy in 2001.

The fall of the Berlin Wall in November 1989 took the world by surprise. It saw bewildered border guards unsure whether to arrest people or join in the euphoria. Germans and tourists alike attacked the concrete wall with pick-axes much to the delight of the international press. Germans themselves had almost given up believing in the possibility of reunification. Berlin was rudely awakened from its forty-five year slumber. Investors and speculators with their western architects – attracted by prime undeveloped sites, encouraged by tax concessions, banking on the attraction of the city's notoriety, historical nostalgia and the likelihood of its rebirth as the capital of a new Berlin Republic – descended like locusts.

Bonn, West Germany's small-town provisional capital for almost half a century, had to relinquish its international role. Politicians reluctantly left its cosy comfort for the harsh economic and social realities of the east. But what style of architecture should the new Berlin Republic adopt? Memories of Hitler's Third Reich had to be expunged. The two houses of the federal parliament (Bundesrat and Bundestag), the federal chancellery (Bundeskanzleramt), federal presidium (Bundespräsidialamt), associated administration and eleven ministries had to be housed. Every building was the subject of international architectural competition.

The Reichstag was one of the few historical landmarks on the west side of the Wall during the Cold War. Hitler saw it as a symbol of the Weimar Republic he had replaced and denounced it as a "gossip shop". After the Soviet army hoisted the Red flag over its ruins in 1945 it was restored, but virtually shunned until Foster and Partners won the international competition to re-style it for use as the new Berlin Republic's parliament, the Bundestag. Foster's first competition design, with an enormous flat glass roof sheltering Wallot's stone structure, was likened to a petrol station canopy. Pressure grew to reinstate the original dome. Foster translated this into a glass dome with internal spiral ramp, from which the public now have a bird's eye view over the city.

Before the Reichstag's transformation began in 1995 many cultural gestures were made to signal Berlin's sensitivity to both the past and the future. Cyrillic graffiti scratched into the Reichstag's stone walls by Soviet soldiers was preserved under glass. A programme of modern art acquisition was planned for the interior and the American–Bulgarian artist Christo was finally allowed to realise his twenty-four year plan to wrap the Reichstag in aluminium coated polypropylene cloth, bound with 15,600 metres of blue rope.

Across a bow in the Spree river, to the west of the Reichstag, Axel Schultes and Charlotte Frank planned an east-west strip of government buildings to symbolically unite the divided city. Their design for the Chancellery, a white pavilion with circular features, was completed in 2001. Berliners, with typical blunt speech and irreverence, dubbed it the "federal washing machine", although it more closely resembles a sheikh's palace or middle eastern airport. From his suite the Federal Chancellor gazes out through bullet-proof windows over three new federal blocks named after Paul Löbe, Marie Elisabeth Lüders and Jakob Kaiser, all members of the last parliament before Hitler gained power.

Young architects have greatly profited from the widespread architectural competition system. Helmut Kleine-Kraneburg and Martin Gruber won the 1995 competition for the Bundespräsidialamt, a solitary elliptical black stone-clad building among trees in the Tiergarten between Schloss Bellevue (the president's official residence) and the victory column on the Strasse des 17 Juni. More modest housing for parliamentarians in the Serpentine, a 500-metre long snaking block of four hundred apartments, was designed by Georg Bumiller.

The cost of both relocating a government and reunifying a country were greatly underestimated. New buildings for some of the eleven ministries that moved from Bonn to Berlin were scrapped in favour of recycling ex-Nazi buildings that had also been used by the GDR. So it is that the Berlin Republic's finance ministry sits in the Nazi's former air ministry, Joseph Goebbel's propaganda ministry has been remodelled by architect Josef Paul Kleihues for the present employment ministry, and architect Hans Kollhoff has exorcised the former Nazi Reichsbank for today's foreign ministry.

Over thirty new embassy buildings have been constructed since 1990 and, because Germany is a federation of sixteen states, every German regional government has also had to build in the capital. The most attractive grouping of foreign delegations is the Nordic Embassies Complex. This village of five embassies, located opposite Gropius' Bauhaus

Archives Museum, was completed by six architects' offices in 1999. International star architects were called on to fly their nation's flags: from Hans Hollein for Austria to Diener & Diener for Switzerland, and from Christian de Portzamparc for France to OMA for the Netherlands. The US embassy on Pariser Platz was delayed while planners and diplomats argued over the width of the security strip around the building.

It is not only government and diplomatic requirements that have had an enormous impact on the city's appearance. There are also the necessary camp followers. The two major political parties, SPD and CDU, have built modern headquarters. The Green Party, in line with its policies, renovated an existing building. After the CDU's financing scandal its glass box was dubbed the "Titanic in aspic". Over six hundred lobbyist organisations, national banks and foreign economic institutions have also gathered in Berlin to rub shoulders with decision-makers.

Few nations, apart from Brazil or Pakistan, have attempted to create instant capitals. Metropoles grow and adapt over centuries. In an attempt to speed up the process Hans Stimmann, appointed Berlin building director in 1991, propagated a "critical reconstruction" of the city. The theory had a close relationship to Rob Krier's infill and repair work in the eighties. Block planning, material and height restrictions were imposed in line with Wilhelminian or Prussian forms, as if the intervening centuries had never taken place.

THE **"Berlin Debate",** THE BATTLE FOR BERLIN'S **ARCHITECTURAL IMAGE,** IMMEDIATELY BROKE OUT AMONG GERMAN AND INTERNATIONAL architects, ACADEMICS, POLITICIANS AND NATIONAL NEWSPAPERS.

Reconstructionists praised Christoph Mäckler's stone-walled Lindencorso on Unter den Linden and modernists, who equated glass with democratic transparency and deconstruction with the true state of a twenty-first century city, supported Günter Behnisch, architect of the last Bundestag building in Bonn. Architects either complied with the official creed in order to get work, were bludgeoned into submission, or fought with bureaucracy for years. In most cases big business won.

Daimler-Benz had been negotiating to buy a piece of Potsdamer Platz, before the Wall fell, as a branch office. They immediately revised and expanded their scheme. Renzo Piano's team of international architects completed 120 shops, offices, banks, a musical theatre, cinemas and a Grand Hyatt in 1998 with little evidence of "critical reconstruction" having hindered progress. Likewise Helmut Jahn produced popular event architecture for the Sony Centre (2001). In contrast Pariser Platz was forced into a kitschy neo-classical straitjacket. Günter Behnisch only obtained planning permission for his Akademie der Künste of glazed clarity in 1998, after years of discussions and revisions. Next door Frank Gehry won through with his DG Bank by hiding his avant garde furore behind a strictly restrained exterior.

But planners were unable to hold back the tide of commercial interest wanting landmark buildings from star architects. In 1994 the *Frankfurter Allgemeine Zeitung* reported that twenty big commercial projects were being developed in just one street, Friedrichstrasse, formerly on the east side of the wall. Jean Nouvel's Galerie Lafayette and Pei Cobb Freed's Passagen, along with the rest of the street's shopping and office developments, have little relationship with each other, let alone "critical reconstruction". Some architects, with supportive clients simply refused to conform. Sauerbruch Hutton's banana yellow GSW Housing Association complex and Nicholas Grimshaw's steel ribbed Ludwig Erhard Haus are uncompromising modern insertions into an existing city structure.

Many Eastern European Jewish families emigrated to Berlin following the lifting of travel restrictions. Previously shrinking Jewish congregations suddenly needed new community buildings. Zvi Hecker's 1995 Heinz Galinski Jewish school was the first to be built in Berlin for over fifty years. Daniel Libeskind's Jewish Museum, planned as merely an extension to Berlin's history museum, attracted both controversy and praise, taking on a life of its own during its long gestation from the 1989 competition to completion in 1999. Millions visited the empty building even before its permanent collections were installed. It is one of Berlin's major attractions along with Eduard Knoblauch's 1866 synagogue, now restored to its gilded and blue splendour on Oranienburger Strasse. All these buildings require round the clock police protection in present day Germany.

Since reunification Berlin has had to be seen to be dealing with its past. Peter Eisenman's Memorial to the Murdered Jews of Europe was fought for by a prominent group of private citizens. Former Berlin mayor Eberhard Diepgen complained the city was filling up with memorials but despite this the project was ratified by government in 1999. Construction may begin in 2002. Peter Zumthor's Topography of Terror museum over the excavated Gestapo cells, which have been exhibited under open sky since 1987, has suffered budget problems and is still in construction. More modest memorials, their necessity hotly debated, have been completed half a century late. In Bebel Platz, on the site of the book burning, artist Micha Ullmann and architect Andreas Zerr have inserted a glass panel in the paving, through which a room of empty bookshelves can be seen below.

Much of Berlin's convalescent architecture goes unnoticed. Berlin's infrastructure, communication and transport systems have all been redesigned. Anticipated pressure on housing led to whole new suburbs along waterways in Overhavel, Rummelsburger Bucht and Biesdorf-Sud. Industrial gems under conservation orders have found new roles. Hamburger Bahnhof, an ex-railway station remodelled by Kleihues, is now the Museum of Contemporary Art. Oberbaum City, an ex-Narva light bulb factory, is a business suburb replanned by Schweger and Partner, with an International Design Zentrum.

Potsdamer Platz was proclaimed Europe's biggest building site but Lehrter Bahnhof, Berlin's central railway station designed by von Gerkan Marg and Partner, will be bigger. This European rail interchange is scheduled for completion in time for the 2006 Football World Cup. Five levels of underground tracks will carry a quarter of a million passengers daily to the edges of the continent. Above ground a 321-metre long glass barrel roof between two tower blocks will dwarf the Bundeskanzleramt across the Spree.

BERLIN'S **METAMORPHOSIS** HAS BEEN radical AND rapid.

Opposing architectural theories and financial interests have fought to control its development. Consequently architecture itself has come under fire but sometimes even old forms are too radical. One of the many reconstruction debates centres on whether Mies van der Rohe's 1926 memorial to the murdered revolutionists Rosa Luxemburg and Karl Liebknecht, demolished by the Nazis in 1933, should be rebuilt. Its defiant inscription, "I am, I was, I will be", still has the power to polarise.

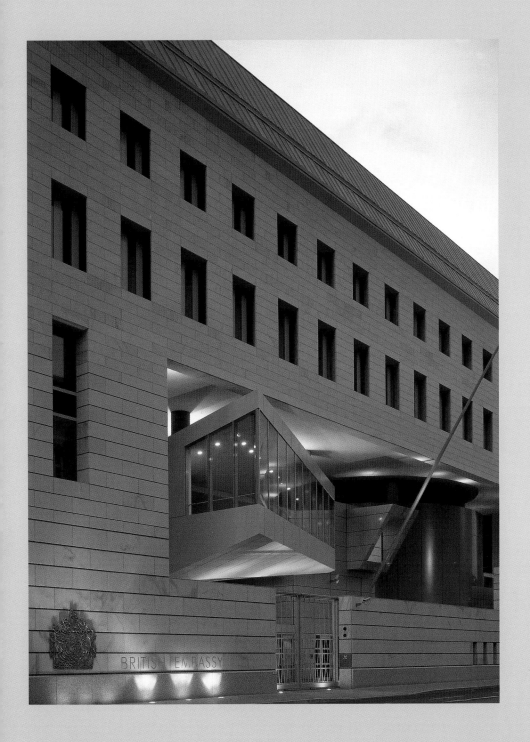

KANT-DREIECK ("SHARK'S FIN)

There is always space in a big city for eccentricity. The "shark's fin" is a 34-ton metal-plated solar energy storage unit which turns according to the sun's position.

REICHSTAG

A building which has weathered far-reaching historical changes and risen like a phoenix in new clothes to represent the new Berlin federal republic of Germany.

NORDIC EMBASSIES/BUNDESKANZLERAMT

One of the most striking and unusual diplomatic solutions. Denmark, Finland, Iceland, Norway and Sweden built a community of embassies behind a copper wall (left). A detail of columns at the Bundeskanzleramt (right).

BAUHAUS ARCHIVES MUSEUM

The Bauhaus Archives building – an administrator for the licensing of Bauhaus designs, plus library and exhibition centre – designed by Walter Gropius.

BUNDESKANZLERAMT

To expunge traces of the Third Reich, the two houses of the federal parliament, the federal chancellery (Bundeskanzleramt), federal presidium and 11 ministries had to be housed. Every building was the subject of international architectural competition.

NEUE NATIONALGALERIE

With this classically planned national art gallery Mies re-imported the Modern movement. The steel and glass pavilion is a temple to the arts on a concrete podium, which also serves as a good skateboarding surface!

EINSTEINTURM/SHELLHAUS

Built for experiments to check Einstein's theory of relativity, the observatory itself has become a cult structure (left). This expressionist office block, planned as a series of waves, was built during a boom in commercial activity before the depression (right).

VELODROME/KARL MARX ALLEE

Two circular metal roofs shelter Prenzlauer Velodrome built in anticipation of Berlin hosting the 2000 Olympics (left). These newly renovated apartments are now in demand for their unusual character and central location (right).

TELECOMS TOWER/PALAST DER REPUBLIK

The recently renovated 365-metre high tower has two viewing platforms and a revolving restaurant in the steel sphere (left). The GDR's parliament, with public restaurants and conference rooms, was considered the height of modernity (right).

BERLIN WALL/KONGRESSHALLE

The city's most famous and hated landmark for 28 years (left). Built as a symbol of German–American friendship, the Kongresshalle in now an international conference and exhibition centre (right).

PHILHARMONIE

Designed from the inside out for perfect acoustics. This expressionist tent acquired its extra skin of gold anodised plate in 1981.

KAISER WILHELM MEMORIAL CHURCH

Built in memory of the Kaiser the bombed ruin is known as "the lipstick" and serves as a war memorial with modern chapel and tower.

BAUHAUS ARCHIVES MUSEUM

After his death Gropius's design, planned for a Darmstadt site, was brought to West Berlin to bolster its image as an internationally important city.

UMLAUFKANAL/RAUCHSTRASSE CITY VILLAS

This research station for the Technical University is an early experiment in colourful high-tech architecture (left). Part of a plan to fill empty sites with modern versions of nineteenth century suburban family villas (right).

SCHÜTZEN QUARTIER/PHILOSOPHISCHES INSTITUT

Reminiscent of his Disney projects, Rossi used the original layout of a ruined block and designed every property individually with post modern details and colour (left). Inken and Hinrich Baller's expressionism breaks with strict modernism (right).

REICHSTAG

When pressure grew to reinstate the Reichstag's original dome, Foster and Partners translated it into a glass dome with internal spiral ramp, from which the public now have a bird's eye view over the city.

BUNDESKANZLERAMT

Official office of the Federal Chancellor, his ministers and 500 civil servants. Nicknamed "the federal washing machine" because of its gleaming whiteness and circular cut-outs.

SERPENTINE

A snaking block of four hundred apartments for members of parliament and employees. Despite the hard uncompromising surroundings all living rooms have south facing panoramic views over the Spree and Tiergarten Park.

NORDIC EMBASSY COMPLEX

One of the most striking and unusual diplomatic solutions. Denmark, Finland, Iceland, Norway and Sweden built a community of embassies behind a copper wall.

SWEDISH EMBASSY/BRITISH EMBASSY

An interior typical of the other four Nordic embassies in this complex in its use of natural finishes and craft work (left). By juggling broken forms and bright colour, Wilford plays down the impact of a high security building (right).

POTSDAMER PLATZ

Daimler-Benz constructed a "city within the city" with flats, shops, offices, banks, a Grand Hyatt Hotel, nineteen cinema screens, musical and variety theatres and a casino.

SONY CENTRE

A water feature under a glass circus tent between towers housing Sony's European headquarters creates a popular public plaza with cafes and restaurants.

DG BANK

Behind this strict facade a glass whale rises from the depths of the building to fill the inner courtyard. "One of the best things I've ever done." said Gehry.

QUARTIER 206/GALERIE LAFAYETTE

More than twenty commercial blocks designed by international star architects have been built in Friedrichstrasse since reunification (left). French flair in a department store designed around an inverted glass funnel (right).

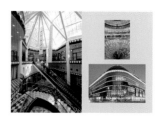

LUDWIG ERHARD HAUS

Fifteen steel arches span a financial exchange and offices. High-tech and morphic architecture, mainly by non-German architects, is bringing new life to the capital's streetscape.

GSW HOUSING ASSOCIATION COMPLEX

A fifties office tower has been refurbished and low level extensions added with passive energy saving systems, sensual shapes and colour.

HEINZ GALINSKI SCHOOL/ORANIENBURGER STRASSE SYNAGOGUE

The first new Jewish school in Berlin since the war is laid out like the petals of a sunflower connected by "snake" corridors (left). Restored as a landmark the synagogue's dome rises over a very lively quarter of Berlin (right).

JEWISH MUSEUM

A silvery metal blitz in the garden of the Berlin Museum, for which it was originally intended as merely an extension. The empty building was a major attraction even before its collection of historical Jewish artefacts was installed.

HAMBURGER BAHNHOF/BERLIN WATERWORKS

This former railway station was renovated for contemporary art. At night its facade is outlined in coloured fluorescent light strips (left). The waterworks demonstrate a different kind of retro-architecture, a return to 20th century expressionist forms (right).

TRIAS

Like ocean liners with their curved prows rising over a train line and canal these green tinted, glass clad, offices raise the quality of a major arterial route into the city centre.

Picture credits

The publishers would like to thank the following sources for their kind permission to reproduce the pictures in this book:

Bibliography

Alexanderplatz: Urban Planning Ideas Competition, (Ernst & Sohn, 1994)

Arts of the Third Reich, Peter Adams (Thames and Hudson, 1992)

Bauwelt Berlin Annual: Chronology of Building Events 1996–2001, (eds) Martina Düttmann, Felix Zwoch (Bauwelt Berlin and Birkhäuser Verlag)

Berlin Brandenburg: An Architectural Guide, Peter Güttler et al (Ernst & Sohn, 1990)

Berlin: Contemporary Architecture Guide, Duane Phillips (Ellipsis London Ltd)

Berlin Morgen, (eds) Vittorio Magnago Lampugnani, Michael Mönninger, Volker Fischer, Anna Meseure (Deutsches Architekur-Museum with Verlag Gerd Hatje, 1991)

Berliner Plätze (Nicolai, 2001)

Berlin Stadtplan (Falk Editions)

Der Neue Potsdamer Platz, Andreas Muhs, Heinrich Wefing (be.bra verlag, 1998)

Deutschland: Architektur im 20 Jahrhundert, (eds) Winfried Nerdinger, Romana Schneider, Wilfried Wang (Deutsches Architektur-Museum with Prestel, 2000)

Ein Stück Grossstadt als Experiment (eds) Vittorio Magnago Lampugnani, Romana Schneider (Deutsches Architektur-Museum with Verlag Gerd Hatje, 1994)

Hitler's State Architecture (Pennsylvania University Press, 1990)

Topography of Terror on the Prinz Albrecht Terrain (ed) Reinhard Rürup (Verlag Willmuth Arenhövel, 1989)